What's That?

ISBN: 9798575478409

6-12-20

What's That?

100 close up photos of everyday items

Can you solve them all or will you be scratching your head trying to work out "what's that"?

All will be revealed at the end of the book with a full sized photo of each object

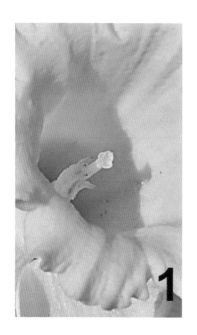

Holidays and outdoors - Answer on page 30

4

Holidays and outdoors - Answer on page 31

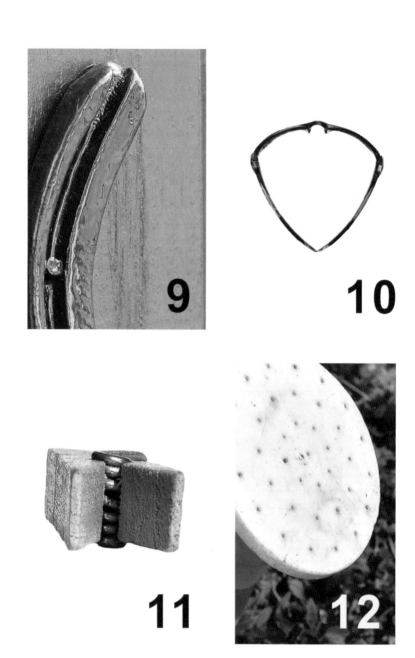

9

10

11

12

Holidays and outdoors - Answer on page 32

13

14

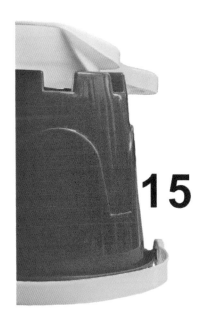

15

16

Holidays and outdoors - Answer on page 33

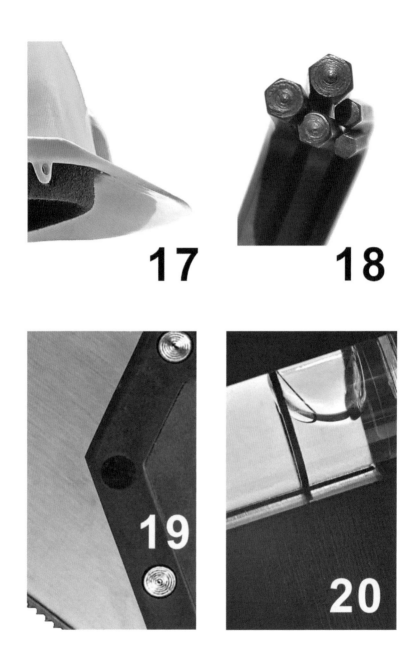

17

18

19

20

DIY - Answer on page 34

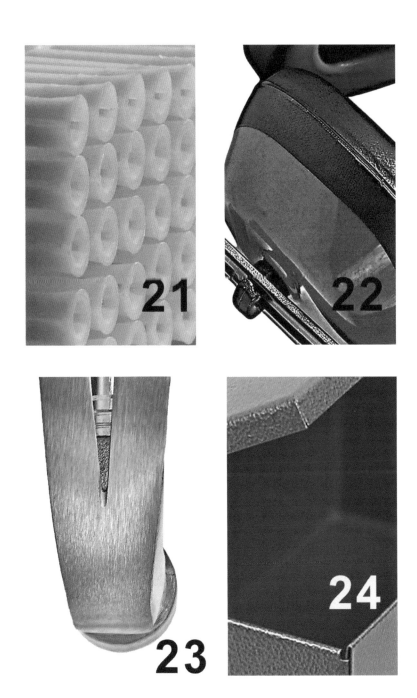

DIY - Answer on page 35

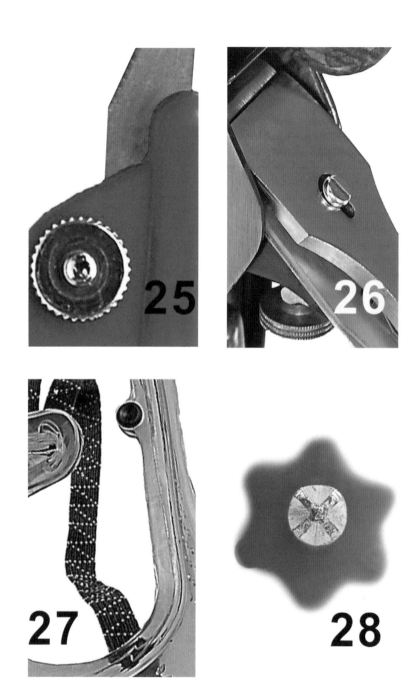

25

26

27

28

DIY - Answer on page 36

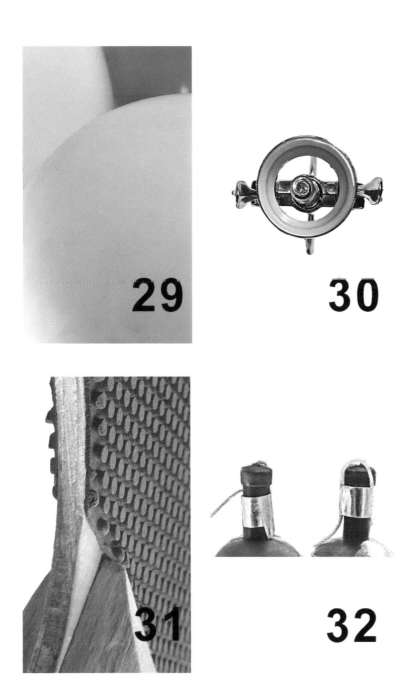

Parties and Games - Answer on page 37

33

34

35

36

Parties and Games - Answer on page 38

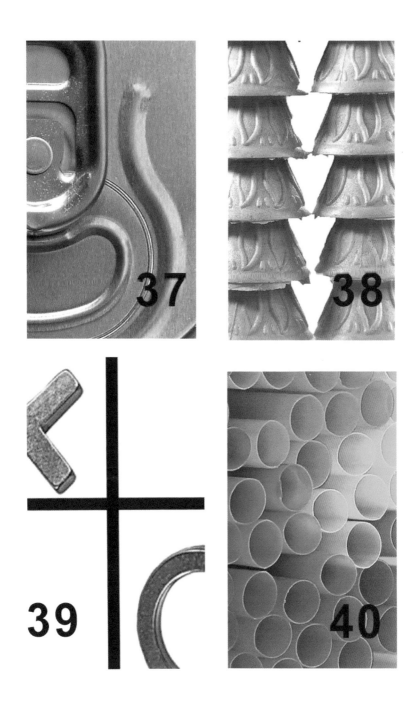

Parties and Games - Answer on page 39

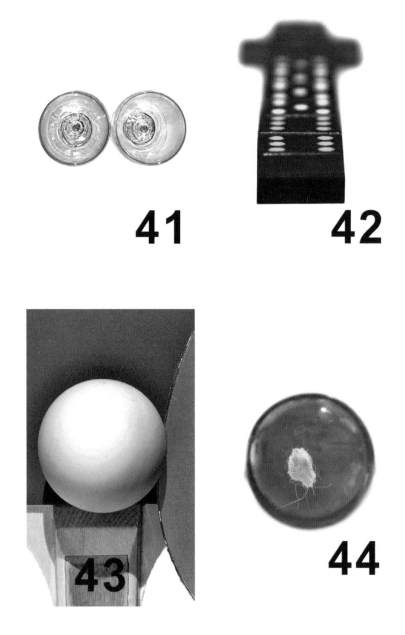

41

42

43

44

Parties and Games - Answer on page 40

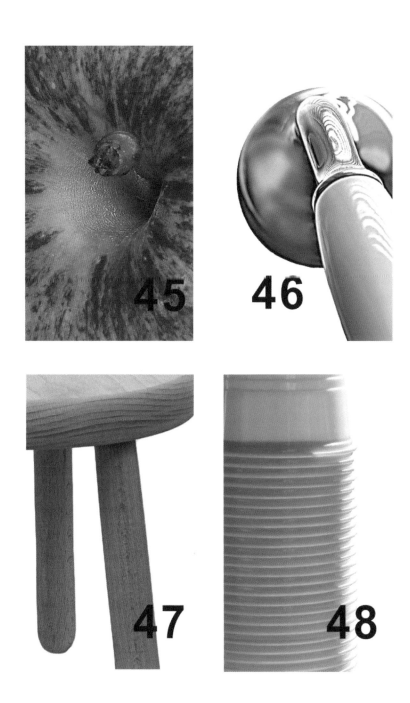

45

46

47

48

Home - Answer on page 41

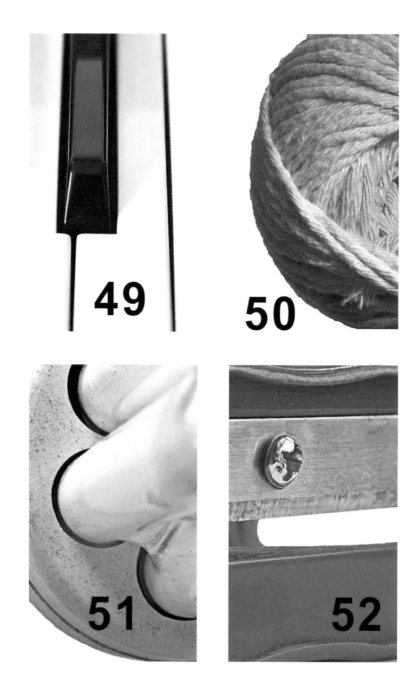

49

50

51

52

Home - Answer on page 42

53

54

55

56

Home - Answer on page 43

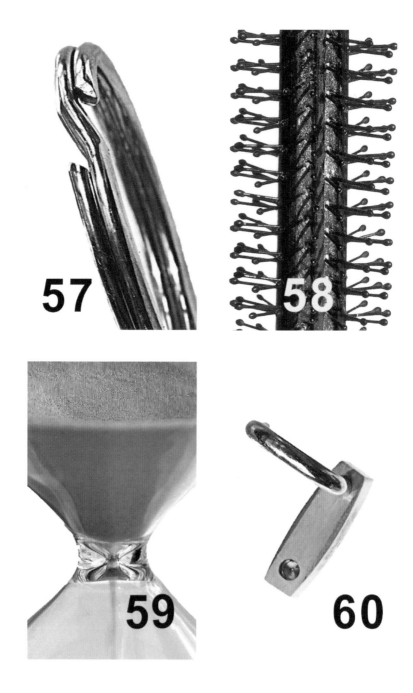

57

58

59

60

Home - Answer on page 44

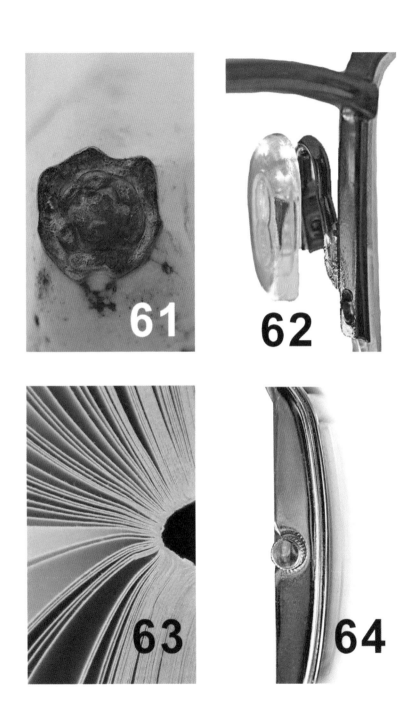

Home - Answer on page 45

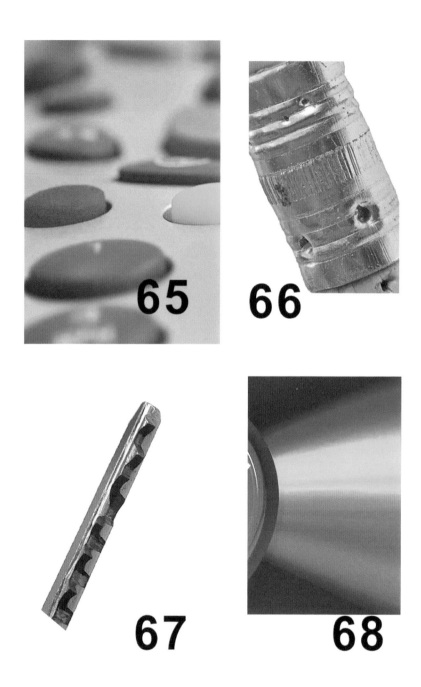

65

66

67

68

Home - Answer on page 46

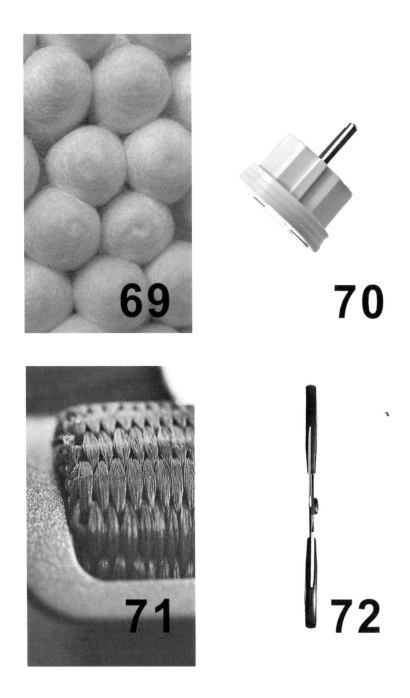

69

70

71

72

Home - Answer on page 47

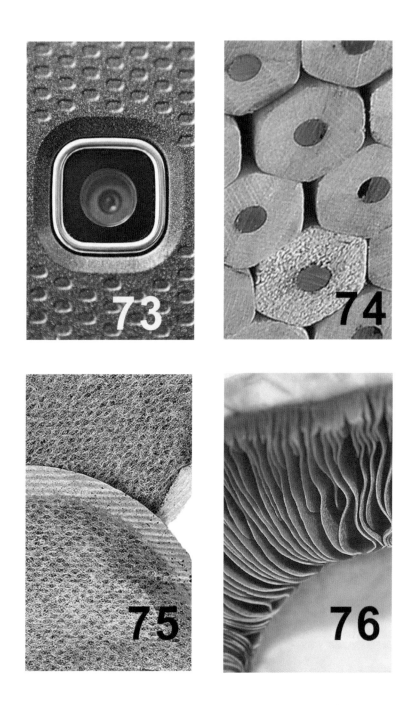

Home - Answer on page 48

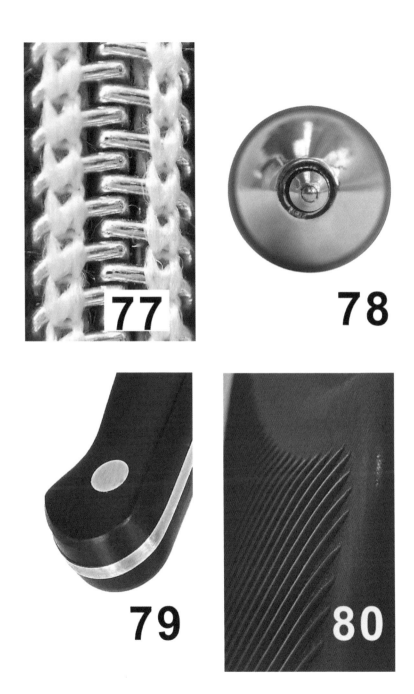

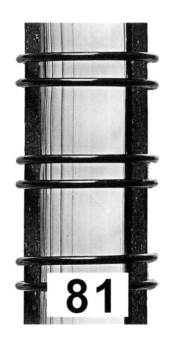

81

82

83

84

Home - Answer on page 50

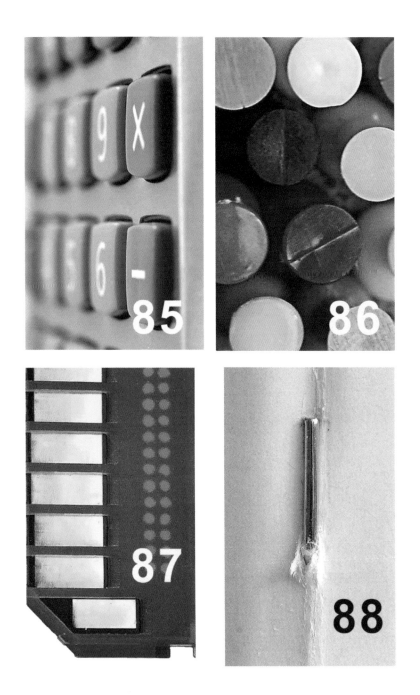

85

86

87

88

Office - Answer on page 51

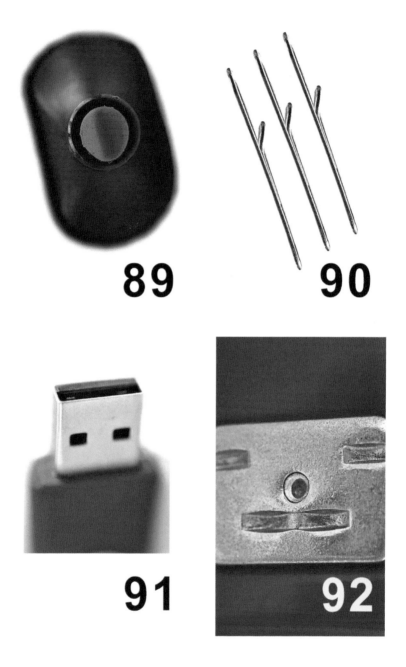

89

90

91

92

Office - Answer on page 52

97   **98**

99   **100**

DIY - Answer on page 54

WHAT'S THAT
ANSWERS

Please be aware that you will see 4 answers on each page

Answer to page 4

5

6

7

8

Answer to page 5

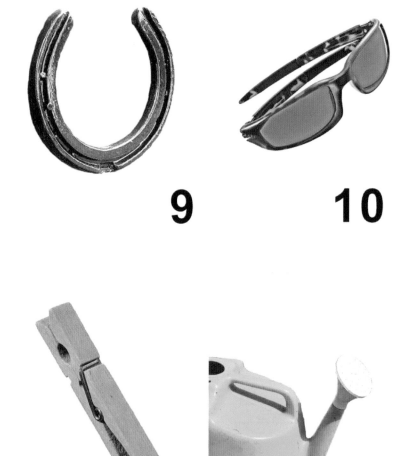

9

10

11

12

Answer to page 6

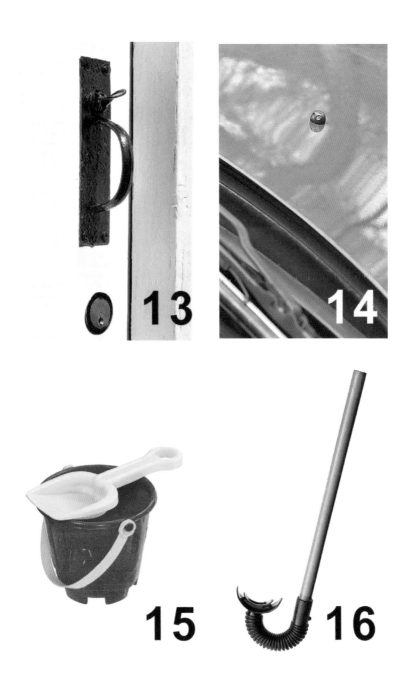

13

14

15

16

Answer to page 7

17

18

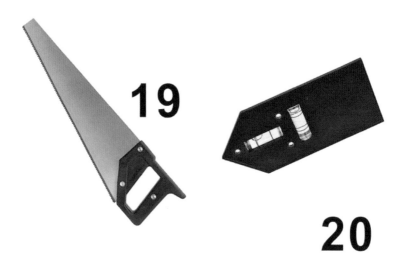

19

20

Answer to page 8

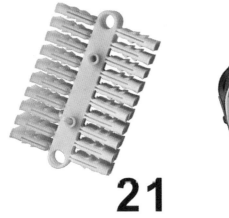

21

22

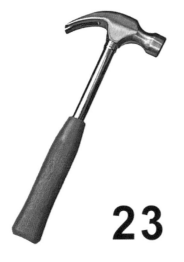

23

24

Answer to page 9

25

26

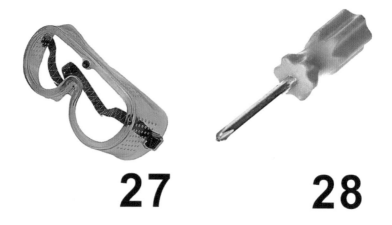

27

28

Answer to page 10

29

30

31

32

Answer to page 11

33

34

35

36

Answer to page 12

37

38

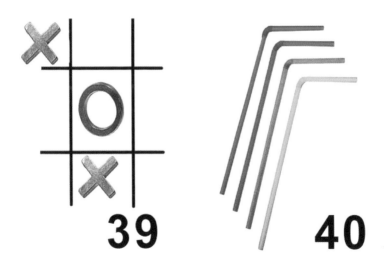

39

40

41

42

43

44

Answer to page 14

45

46

47

48

Answer to page 15

49

50

51

52

Answer to page 16

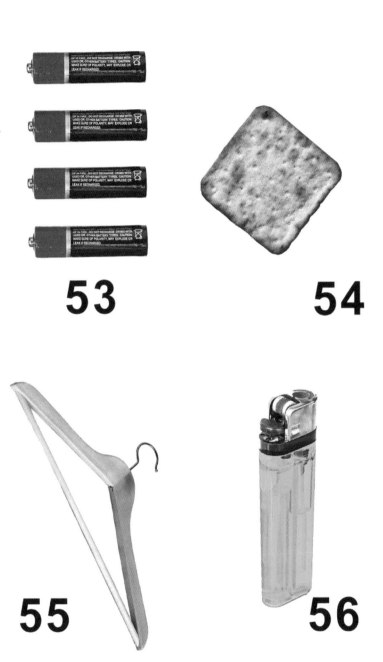

53

54

55

56

Answer to page 17

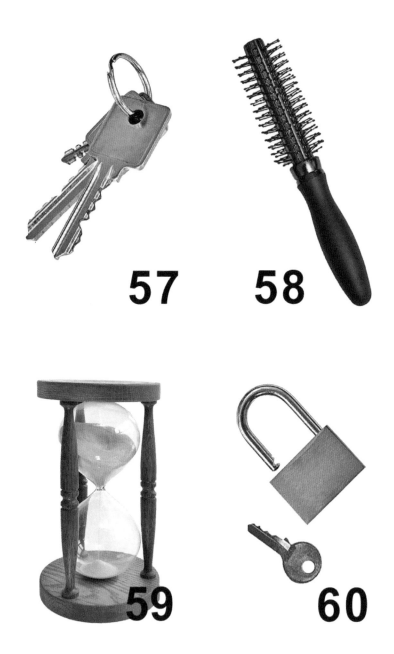

57

58

59

60

Answer to page 18

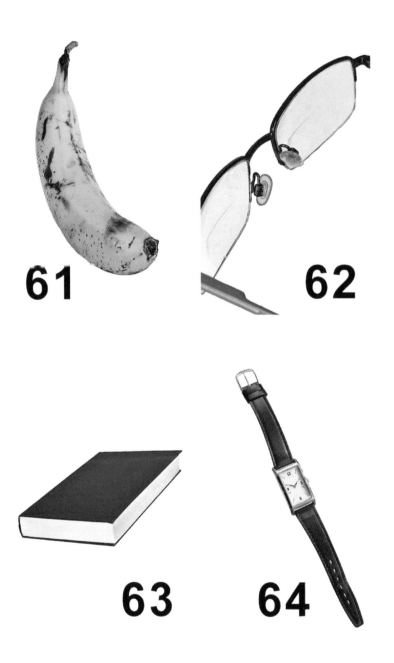

61

62

63

64

Answer to page 19

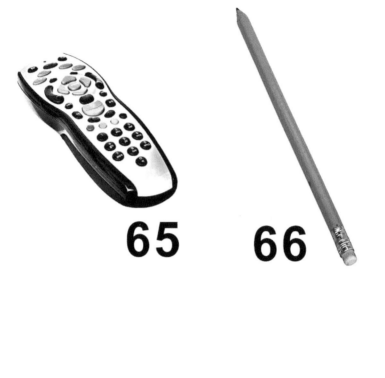

65

66

67

68

Answer to page 20

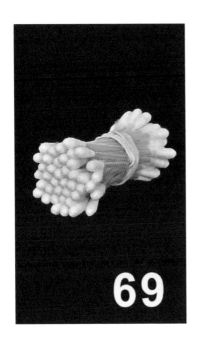

69

70

71

72

Answer to page 21

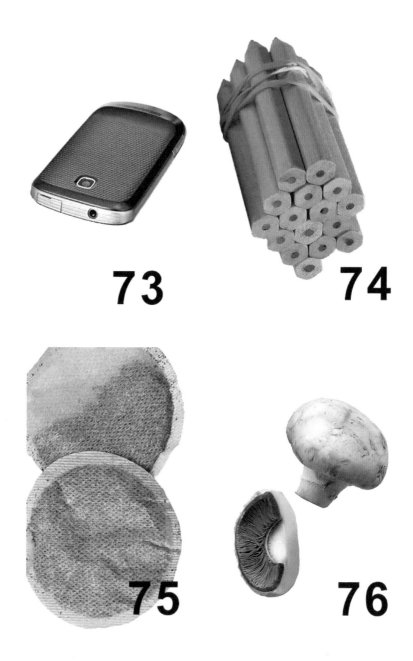

73

74

75

76

Answer to page 22

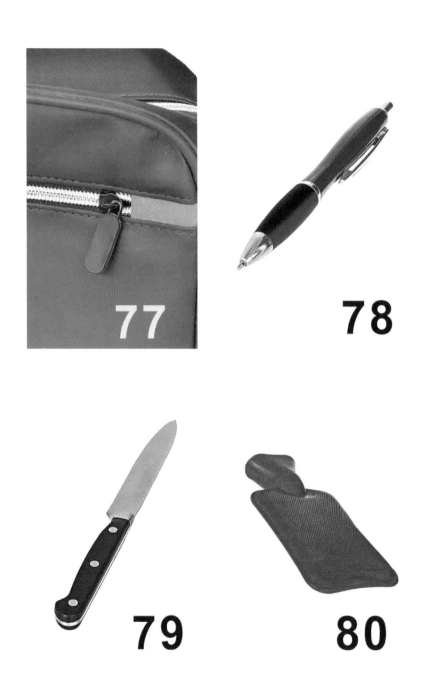

77

78

79

80

Answer to page 23

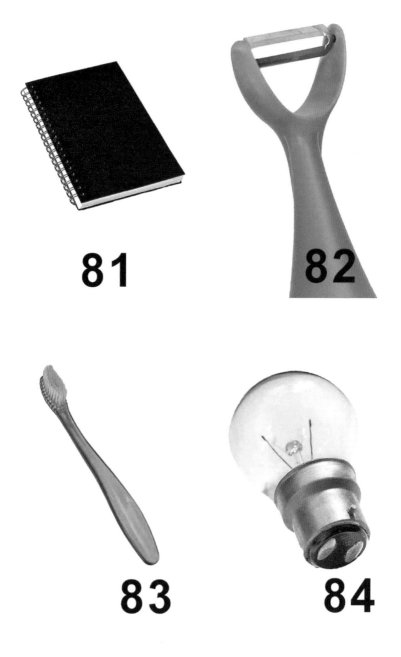

81

82

83

84

Answer to page 24

85

86

87

88

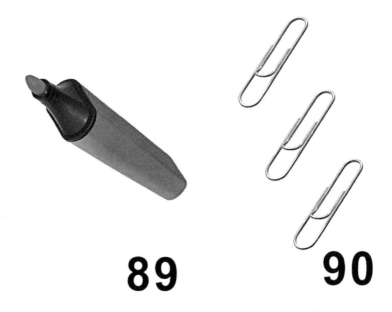

89

90

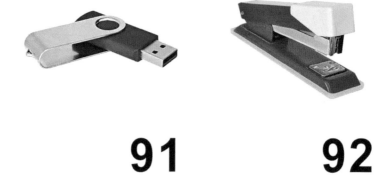

91

92

Answer to page 26

93

94

95

96

Answer to page 27

97

98

99

100

Answer to page 28

Answers

1. Daffodil
2. Beach huts
3. Sundial
4. Telescope
5. Water fountain
6. Binoculars
7. Plant pots
8. Sombrero
9. Horseshoe
10. Sunglasses
11. Clothes bag
12. Watering can
13. Door handle latch
14. Car windscreen nozzle
15. Bucket and spade
16. Swimming snorkel
17. Hard hat

18. Allen keys
19. Saw
20. Spirit level
21. Wall plugs
22. Ear defenders
23. Hammer
24. Toolbox
25. Craft knife
26. Wood plane
27. Safety goggles
28. Screwdriver
29. Balloons
30. Bottle opener
31. Table tennis bat
32. Party poppers
33. Champagne bottle
34. Golf ball and tee
35. Thimble
36. Party whistle

37. Drinks can
38. Ice cream cones
39. Noughts and crosses, tic-tac-toe
40. Drinking straws
41. Wine glasses
42. Dominoes
43. Table tennis bat and ball
44. Candle
45. Apple
46. Showerhead
47. Wooden stool
48. Plastic drinks cups
49. Piano keys
50. Ball of string
51. Electric light bulb
52. Pencil sharpener
53. Batteries
54. Cracker

55. Clothes hanger
56. Lighter
57. Keyring
58. Hairbrush
59. Hourglass
60. Padlock
61. Banana
62. Glasses
63. Book pages
64. Wristwatch
65. TV remote
66. Pencil
67. Key
68. CD disk
69. Cotton buds
70. Plug adapter
71. Strap buckle
72. Scissors
73. Mobile phone lens

74. Pencils
75. Teabags
76. Mushrooms
77. Zip
78. Ballpoint pen
79. Knife
80. Hot water bottle
81. Spine of the book
82. Vegetable cleaner
83. Toothbrush
84. Electric light bulb
85. Calculator
86. Pins
87. Memory card
88. Staples
89. Highlighter
90. Paper clips
91. USB stick
92. Stapler

93. Car headlight
94. Seaside shell
95. Outdoor light
96. Bird box
97. Pliers
98. Drill key
99. Measure
100. Bench vice

OTHER BOOKS BY LES DALE

Grandma's Little Black Book of Recipes - from 1910

More of Grandma's Little Black Book of Recipes - from 1905 - 1927

A Quiz A Week - for Enthusiasts and Quizmasters

A Quiz A Week - with Joker Rounds

Runner 267

Five Hundred Reasons

Growing up in Hope

If you've enjoyed this book, please leave a review

Thanks, Les

Printed in Great Britain
by Amazon

26179088R00037